A
Sacred Sex
Devotional

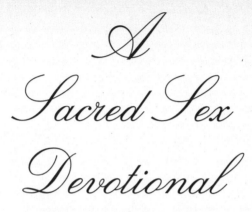

A Sacred Sex Devotional

365 INSPIRING THOUGHTS TO ENHANCE INTIMACY

Edited by Rafael Lorenzo

Park Street Press
Rochester, Vermont

Park Street Press
One Park Street
Rochester, Vermont 05767
www.InnerTraditions.com

Park Street Press is a division of Inner Traditions International

Library of Congress Cataloging-in-Publication Data

A Sacred sex devotional : 365 inspiring thoughts to enhance
intimacy / edited by Rafael Lorenzo.
         p. cm.
    ISBN 0-89281-935-9 (alk. paper)
     1. Sex—Quotations, maxims, etc. 2. Sex—Literary collections.
I. Lorenzo, Rafael.

    PN6084.S49 S23 2000
    306.7—dc21   00-062330

Printed and bound in Canada

10 9 8 7 6 5 4 3 2 1

Text design by Priscilla Baker, layout by Rachel Goldenberg
Typeset in Bernhard Modern with Lucia as a display face

Introduction

What has happened to the language of lovers? Where are the rich, sensual, erotic, and alluring words that can describe our feelings and emotions? For centuries in cultures throughout the world there have been poetic and evocative words used to express the ecstatic feelings that men and women share in that marvelous and mysterious moment of being in love. For people who want to find their way back to that moment, this book contains inspirations that reveal the sacred tradition of ecstasy in love and sexuality.

Our understanding of the sacredness of sexuality is rooted in the qualities of love and devotion that emerge from a sense of the world as a divine affair—a unified Cosmos—held together by forces originating in the generative power of creation itself. This cosmic understanding implicit in a sacred notion of sexuality perceives the wholeness of things in the relationships of correspondence between the outward universal and the inward particular. Thus, qualities of the cosmos reflect us— have character and mood and feeling that are reflected in us—and we, reciprocally, are a symbolic setting and landscape expressive of natural forces. The lover is the microcosmic individual, the finite one contained in the infinite, macrocosmic All, and it is through the mystical bonding power of love that he or she experiences a unity with the infinite.

In sacred sexuality divine and cosmic forces at work actually emanate from the beloved. The world of sacred sexuality is a garden, a paradise, a land of milk and honey. The elements earth, air, fire, wood, and water (and their worldly manifestations as river, rain, mountain, trees, sky, and elemental qualities of hot and cold) manifest the "higher" and "lower" form and power of these cosmic forces at work in nature, suffusing completely into the terms of the lover's situation both as fact and as consciousness. In the four seasons we find the essence of cosmic rhythms manifested in the changes appearing in the very qualities of the physical world. The changing qualities of the seasons and the natural setting itself become the changing qualities of our devotional love and desire. The selections in this book, therefore, have been organized according to seasonal qualities of relationship, reflecting the many moods and levels of intensity of love and sexuality: the newness of spring, the expansiveness of Summer, the maturation of Fall, the inwardness of Winter.

Through its powerful alchemy, sexuality connects the crude substance of material reality with the sublime substance of the spiritual. That this connection is already there, latently, within our living physical body, is the crucial secret that sexual love in its special intimate way actualizes for human beings. For, what is latent in the universe is latent in us also. We stand in a privileged position, being ensouled and conscious, able to bear witness to the experience of our being at any given moment. Through our sexual nature's latent power, we discover the doors in this world—within us—that open to the source of all the other worlds and even to the fount of Creation itself. Everything we are, everything we do, everything we see, speaks to us in its very appearance the message of love as the message of self-transcendence. Sexuality is a special ground of resonance for our connection with cosmic forces and offers a privileged zone for Creation's appearance to happen in the nature of our lives.

In the mystery of sexual love, language becomes a poetry of evocation and charm, and the merely symbolic becomes the vehicle of real change that love's mystical process evokes. The language of love and desire as ordinary language becomes a language of mystical union, a language of worshipful adoration, a language of spiritual ritual and invocation. It is here that the reader may discover in the perennial magic of love's magic words the royal road to the enhancement of intimacy—where the cosmic can manifest in the individual and the eternal emerge in an instant, where separate two, can unite as one.

Spring

The newness of appearance, the shyness, the peeking out of new love like a bud, ripeness, readiness. The world is expectant, open; elaborately coiffed, majestically gowned, and perfumed with flowers and hope. Desire is a dream, a journey of devotion through storms, over mountains and through deserts, to an ecstatic resolution. The air is fresh, and life frolics and sings of its unbridled joy in being. Sexuality is the experiencing of this paradise of the alchemy of love and desire; it is the romance of a magical seeing, a mutual knowing, a reaching out and an attaining. It is the moment when the sun rises and the eyes meet, and the body becomes a new and beautiful world.

One night in the darkness, I demanded
my heart again from thy tresses. I beheld
thy cheek, and drank the cup of thy mouth.
I drew quickly to my breast, and thy tresses
blazed in flame; I pressed lip to lip, and gave
for thy ransom my soul and heart.

Haféz

$\mathcal{L}$overs need to explore more than each other's bodies. They need to plunge into each other's psyches and soar to the heights of the spirit.

Nik Douglas and
Penny Slinger

My heart craves the kiss of your love, my soul thirsts for the most intimate embrace joining me to you.

Saint Gertrude

$\mathscr{A}$h, everything was blessed and beautified by her presence. Wherever I looked, whatever I touched, the rug before her chair, her cushion, her little table—they were all mysteriously allied to her. And, oh, the first time she addressed me by name, that she came so close to me that her innocent breath touched my listening being!

Friedrich Holderlin

*C*ome, south wind recalling love.

Breathe on my garden,

let aromas swell in the air,

my love will graze among the flowers.

St. John of the Cross

$\mathcal{T}$o eat of the trees of the garden is not a luxury merely, but a necessity, as life and vitality depend upon it. When once the laws of Eden are observed, the whole human race will attain a vitality that shall surpass our wildest dream.

John S. Bayne

When a boy and girl experience their first kiss, they find love's oneness, a feeling so strong that they can no longer see each other's faults. The kiss is the gateway to bliss and amorous experience. The kiss provokes erotic ardor, agitates the heart, and is an incitation to the natural gift of self.

Kama Sutra

I do not believe the beauty of another lady can equal hers, because the rose, when it blooms, is no fresher than she; her body is well made and of gracious proportions, and her eyes and her mouth are the light of the world. For never did beauty know how to do more for her, and has so well placed in her all its power that nothing is left to it for others.

Raimon de Miraval

O bee,

in your vast fields

are the lilies as sweet

as the mouth of this girl?

Manikkavacakar

The river of life flows through the

meadows of Eden,

And the meadows of Eden are below her

garment,

The moon is beneath her mantle.

Her body is a song of colors:

Carnation of roses answers to silver,

Black ripe berries

And new-cut sandal wood

Are one note.

The man who takes her is more blessed

Than the God who gave her;

And He is continually called Blessed.

The Thousand and One Nights

In the beginning the first male and the first female stood on the rainbow bridge of heaven and watched the lightning lance thrust down into the waters of chaos. The foam around the jeweled lance solidified to become the first island. Soon the first male and the first female learned how to imitate the act of creation with their own bodies, and from them came the whole world.

Japanese creation myth

The mystic teachings of the East recognize the force of Heaven and Earth as the two fundamental principles that pervade everything. These two forces are operative throughout the phenomenal world: light and dark, hot and cold, dry and wet. They are interdependent and mutually sustaining. The Force of Heaven determines the structure of the male sex organ, whereas the Force of the Earth creates the shape of the female sex organ. The esoteric function of sexual love is the resolution of the complementary intelligences of Heaven and Earth.

Nik Douglas and
Penny Slinger

*A*nd down his mouth comes to

my mouth! and down

His bright dark eyes come over me,

like a hood

Upon my mind! his lips meet mine,

and a flood

Of sweet fire sweeps across me, so I drown.

D. H. Lawrence

$\mathcal{K}$iss me again, kiss me again and again

Give me one of your tastiest kisses

Give me one of your most passionate kisses

And I'll pay you back with four that are

    hotter than fire.

Oh, did that hurt? I'll ease that pain

By giving you ten more of sweetness

    unending.

So as we mingle our kisses with our rapture

We'll take our bliss of each other at our ease.

                  Louise Labé

And in this pout I snatch and capture

That in the ecstasy of rapture,

When the odorous red-rose petals part

That my lips may find their way to the heart

Of the rose of the world, your lips, my rose.

Arthur Symons

Spring has come and the flowers are

    brilliant with color,

Responding to the rhythms of love, your

    supple body moves.

Opening, opening is that most Precious Bud;

My drops of dew help your Peony bloom.

Chang Sheng

In her is the lyre,

in her is the rose,

in her is the harmonious science,

in her we breathe

the vital perfume of all things.

Rubén Darío

There from the love thoughts,

Longings and love words,

Sprang beautiful trees and flowers.

Little streams gurgled through the forests;

Leaping waterfalls foamed;

Great rivers flowed to the sea;

Fish abounded;

Buffalo roamed the plains

And through the wood-paths

Sped all the wild things

Of a new world.

Native American (Okanagon)
creation song

I sing the great joy of singing you,

The great joy of having or not having you,

The frankness of waiting for you, the

    innocence of knowing you,

You who erase all oblivion, hope, and

    ignorance,

Who erases absence and brings me into the

    world.

I sing for the sake of singing, I love you for

    singing

The mystery where love creates me and sets

    itself free.

                    Paul Éluard

*M*arke how the bashfull morne, in vaine

Courts the amorous Marigold,

With sighing blasts, and weeping raine;

Yet she refuses to unfold.

But when the Planet of the day,

Approacheth with his powerful ray,

Then she spreads, then she receives

His warmer beams into her virgin leaves.

                                        Thomas Carew

It sprouts, it sprouts, it is the lettuce he
    watered,
In the garden of deep shade, bending down
    his neck, my darling of his mother,
My one who fills the grain in their furrows
    with beauty, he watered,
My apple tree becoming fruit at its top, it is
    the garden he watered.

                      Sumerian bridal song

The splendor of her body is like a garland of champaka flowers,

Her choice green raiment is like fresh tamil leaves,

Her thighs are like beautiful banana trees, her feet like

Red lotuses, her waist recall the lion's, her gait the swans,

Her jewels are like many flowers of various colors,

Her anklets and her bracelets are like murmuring birds,

Her hands like young buds of mango,
Her breasts like bel fruits, her bodice a mesh
   of creepers,
Her face is like a lotus and her eyebrows
   humming bees,
Her eyes are blossoming fresh blue lotuses,
Her voice is a cuckoo and her actions lovely
   peacocks and parrots,
Her laughter like white flowers and her
   sports the gentle breeze.

                              Tulsi Das

*B*eneath the gold of your dress is hidden
The soul of the wood of a true Breton.
Lady filled with all that counts!
Show us heaven and the gateway.

Tristan Corbiere

*A*t the sudden sight of his beloved, the
heart of a lover should tremble.

Andreas Capellanus

Wherever I look

in this whole world,

a flowering creeper appears

with black carp, red fruit,

golden bangles

and two lovely breasts.

                              Manikkavacakar

The appeal of beauty to passion and passion to beauty was not intended to be a short-lived or limited thing, but to make life last and to last for life. Our sex life ought to be a perpetual fountain of purity and health diffusing its vitality and fragrance through our whole being.

John S. Bayne

Do not dig a canal, let me be your canal,

Do not plough a field, let me be your field,

Farmer, do not search for a wet place,

Let me be your wet place!

Babylonian song

I clasp my hands, my sleeve:

Dew and perfume and color.

If he flowered on a branch

I would plant him

And love him every

Lonely hour.

Geisha song

Ai-yai, Ai-yai,
The bush-bird she has learned to fly.

She sat on her nest, so tightly pressed,
Until her feathers were caressed,
All the feathers of her breast.

Ai-yai, Ai-yai,
The bush-bird she has learned to fly.

She rose from her lonely nest,
Up and up with a mounting zest,
Until she flew her very best.

Ai-yai, Ai-yai,

The bush-bird she has learned to fly.

Song of the Idoma tribe of Nigeria

*L*ove is in the rising of these stars

And desire in the blowing of this wind.

Ibn Zaidun

We slip beneath the silken covers,

All warm and scented; our moment comes,

The dew falls, the Precious Flower opens

In the tenderness of love; the Clouds

and the Rain complete us, complete us.

Huang Ching

Freshness of love is a soft fruit of passion.

Ibn Zaidun

$\mathcal{S}$weet fields of life which death's foote

    dare not presse,

Flowerd with th'unbroken waves of my loves

    brests.

Her body doth present these fields of peace

Where soules are feasted with the soule of

    ease.

               George Chapman

*I*n those times when Nature in powerful

zest

Conceived each day monstrous children,

I'd have loved to live near a young giantess,

A voluptuous cat at the feet of a queen.

I would have loved to see her body flower

with her soul,

To grow up freely in her prodigious play;

To find if her heart bred some dark flame

Amongst the humid mists swimming in

her eyes;

To run leisurely over her marvelous lines;

To creep along the slopes of her enormous
    knees,

And sometimes in summer, when impure
    suns

Made her wearily stretch out across the
    countryside,

To sleep carelessly in the shadow of her
    breasts.

Like a peaceful village at the foot of a
    mountain.

Charles Baudelaire

$\mathscr{S}$he is the sun whose sunset is a screen

Her rising is from the neck of a dress

A branch that sucked the water of youth

Love rained on it and hope harvested it

She sways in the soft fold of the belt

And she looks with a soft turn of the eye

She emerges from behind the chaste shawl

And unveils beneath the scarf of modesty

She appeared among coevals as fine modesty

Of stars adorning unadorned beauty

They went honoring the hill garden as

A ripening garden of youth's strength

And some stems bent with the wind and

Some stems bent with seduction

Some blooms were bedewed with musk

    Some flowers were dripping with dew

A shower of rain pledged protection and

    Their meadow did not rest in weariness

A pasture of love fresh for the taking.

Ibn Zaidun

*E*very beloved object is the center of a

Paradise.

Novalis

O my luve's like a red, red rose,
That's newly sprung in June;
O my luve's like the melodie
That's sweetly played in tune.

As fair art thou, my bonnie lass,
So deep in luve am I;
And I will luve thee still, my dear,
Till a' the seas gang dry.

Till a' the seas gang dry, my dear,

And the rocks melt wi' the sun;

O I will love thee still, my dear,

While the sands o' life shall run.

And fare thee weel, my only luve,

And fare thee weel awile!

And I will come again, my luve,

Though it were ten thousand mile.

Robert Burns

Bow thyself down in adoration,
O angel, at the door of the tavern of love,
for therein kneaded the clay from which
mankind hath been moulded. When sur-
passing beauty hath annihilated a world of
lovers, a fresh world springeth up to love
from the Invisible.

Haféz

An hundred years should go to praise
Thine Eyes, and on thy Forehead Gaze.
Two hundred to adore each Breast:
But thirty thousand to the rest.
An Age at least to every part,
And the last Age should show your Heart.
For Lady you deserve this State;
Nor would I love at lower rate.

                                    Andrew Marvell

*L*ove is a most precious guest; when it enters the soul, there is a very wonderful triumph there; the bridegroom there embraces his beloved bride, and the hallelujah of paradise sounds.

Jacob Böhme

*I*n choosing a lover you are choosing your destiny.

Mantak Chia

She is a waterlily, rich in honey

that grows in forest ponds

and I am the new moon

that climbs high in the sky

and makes her bloom

with his steady light.

Manikkavacakar

*T*he significant feature of the Garden [of Eden] is its loveliness and isolation. They are in a world of their own. No one intrudes, and there is no one to intrude. The nakedness of which they are unashamed is the nakedness of two. If there were more than two, it would not be Eden. It is the impossibility of intrusion that makes it Eden. Into the true Eden there is a certain impossibility of intrusion. This is a true marriage.

John S. Bayne

When the cool breeze wafts from your land, it seems to me I breathe in a wind from paradise, because of the love of my comely girl who has caused me to submit to her, and to whom I have given my passion and my heart. For I have quit all women for her, she has enchanted me so.

Bernart de Ventadour

Happy is he who embraces her

He is first among all lovers.

When she is seen leaving her house

She is like the appearance of the Unique.

Chester Beatty Papyrus

$\mathcal{Y}$ou have the eyes of Hera,

the hands of Athena,

the breasts of Aphrodite.

Blessed is the man who looks upon you.

Thrice blessed is the man who hears you

talk.

A demi-god is the man who kisses you.

A god the man who takes you into bed.

Rutinos

As the Virgin, woman takes the surrendering role and man acts as the initiator. She is the "clean slate" on which he writes the Karmic message, while she confers and shares her untouchable "pure essence" with him alone. In this role, she embodies conventional love at its most potent level. She is the "pure flower" whose fragrance is his alone to smell.

As the Whore, a woman is in the active role; it is she who acts as the initiatress into the mysteries of love. Without any shame or restraint, she is free to give all of herself to him without any restrictions. In this role woman embodies unconventional love. Sure of her sexuality, she offers herself in service without reservation, guilt, or insecurity. She must draw on her own special qualities and confer them on her lover. She is pure Shakti, the power principle of initiation, the High Priestess.

Nik Douglas and
Penny Slinger

To harmonize the mood between lovers, the man should seize her delicate waist and fondle her jadelike body. Talking of being bound together, with one heart and a single intent, they should embrace and kiss, suck tongues, press close and caress each other's ears and head. Soothing above and stimulating below, the many coquetries are revealed. Then the woman should take his Jade Stalk in her left hand, while he strokes her Jade Gate with his right; moved by the life-force of the female element, his Jade

Stalk becomes excited; stimulated by the life force of the male element, her Jade Gate begins to bubble over, like a stream flowing into a valley.

Taoist master Tung

*L*ove is sacred, and sex is sacred, too. The two things are not apart; they belong together.

Lame Deer

*O*nly through sexual union are new beings capable of existing. This union, therefore, represents a place between two worlds, a point of contact between being and nonbeing, where life manifests itself and incarnates the divine spirit.

Alain Daniélou

O, that he would kiss me with the kisses of his mouth! For your love is better than wine, your anointing oils are fragrant, your name is oil poured out; therefore all the maidens love you. Draw me after you, let us make haste.

The Song of Solomon

In an orchard under hawthorn leaves
    the lady holds her lover by her side
    until the watchman cries: it is the dawn.
O God, O God, the dawn! it comes so soon.

Would to God the darkness were not ending,
    and my lover were not leaving me,
    and the watchman saw no day or dawn.
O God, O God, the dawn! it comes so soon.

Fair, sweet friend, kiss me and I'll kiss you
    in the meadow where songbirds sing,
    let's so all this despite the jealous one.
O God, O God, the dawn! it comes so soon.

Fair, sweet friend, let's play a fresh game

   in the garden where songbirds sing;

   until the watchman sounds his bell.

O God, O God, the dawn! it comes so soon.

In the sweet wind that comes from there

   from my fair, courteous, happy friend,

   I've drunk the sweet light of his breath.

O God, O God, the dawn! it comes so soon.

        Anonymous woman troubadour

$\mathscr{S}$he who holds the *sahaja* [quality of naturalness] is fresh and young, and able to wound with the arrows of her sharp glances. She possesses all the marks of beauty, and the clothes and jewels on her body are brightly colored. Her lips are full of nectar, and her body such that a golden creeper cannot compose with it. This type of *nayika* [pure essence, quality] is a *sahaja-nayika* [pure natural essence]: serve such one, and know her excellence and greatness.

Nigurdhartha-prakasavali

Her body is silk like water,

With the curves of water,

Pure and restful as water.

To be with her in the night!

Her hair, the wings of night,

And her hands the pale stars of night.

The Thousand and One Nights

You have burnt my heart and reduced it
to a powder, and made it into kohl for
your eyes;

You have spilt my blood and made it into
henna for your feet.

Stone me with apples; a sweet tongue has
wounded me!

Your sweet wine has driven me mad, and
you have imprisoned me within your
breast.

Ohannes

*O*ften bursts of anger arise between lovers. In this condition love often turns to hate, since nothing can satisfy their longing for each other, and in a wondrous way, out of desire springs hate, and out of hate, desire. Yet beyond measure, beyond nature even, fire gathers strength in water, in that the flame of love burns more fiercely through their opposition than it could through their being at peace.

Richard of St. Victor

The electric corolla I unfold today

offers the nectary of a garden of wives;

in my flesh I surrender to his birds of prey

a whole swarm of rose-colored doves.

Delmira Agustini

*Y*our body is more fit for love than war.
Let heroes wage war; devote yourself to love
at all times.

Ovid

I cannot live a moment without you;
Kissing your face, I sip the lotus sweet juice.

Guntari

*M*y body turns transparent
Waiting for him,
The breeze of his coming
Plays on the sand of my heart.

O night beside him!
O tired lips leeching wine,
Achieving honey,
Knowing at last Spring!

The Thousand and One Nights

I no longer have any power over myself since the day she allowed me to look into her eyes, into that mirror that so delights me.

Bernart de Ventadour

Caressing above and patting below, kissing to the east and nibbling to the west, a thousand charms are revealed and a hundred cares forgotten.

Chinese sexual yoga classic

When Sun's halo is my halo
You are looking at me.
As Hopi maidens mate with
   Traveler-on-Earth
You are looking at me.
As she now gazed at my headplume
   and thrilled
You are looking at me.
As the pollen of my headplume
   dizzied her
You are looking at me.

As her mind with her body is given into
   my hand
You are looking at me.
As I have changed into Jimson-Weed
   Young Man
You are looking at me.
As sun's flexible plume is my plume
You are looking at me.
When sun's halo is my halo
You are looking at me.

                   Native American (Hopi) song

$\mathcal{F}$rom the sand, from everywhere, the

magic arises.

The thunder strikes the ground.

It shakes the women.

It shakes the women to their very eyes.

They look sideways with their eyes.

They gaze about them and they see the father.

Copulate with them!

Eat their vulvas!

Ejaculate into them!

Make them wet!

After cohabiting with them, he hits

their legs.

He walks with a springy step.

He is happy.

The wombs of the women shiver with

excitement.

Their hearts shiver.

The incantation has done all this to them.

Aboriginal "love magic" chant

She demands it, she demands it, she
   demands the bed,
The bed that rejoices the heart,
She demands it, she demands the bed;
The bed that makes the embrace delicious,
   she demands it,
She demands the bed,
She demands the bed of kingship, she
   demands it; she
Demands the bed of queen-ship, she
   demands it;
By him making it delicious, by him
   making it

Delicious, by the delicious bed;
By the bed that makes the embrace
    delicious, by him making it delicious;
By his delicious bed of the delicious
    embrace.

> Babylonian bridal hymn

*W*hat can he know of the fruits of
Paradise, who hath never kissed the apple
of a beauty's cheek?

> Haféz

*M*y breath
　　is here
My bones
　　are here
My flesh
　　is here

I seek you with them
I find you with them

　　Speak to me
　　Say something to me
　　　　　　Native American (Inuit) song

$\mathscr{A}$bstinence sows sand all over

The ruddy limbs and flaming hair

But Desire Gratified

Plants fruits of life & beauty there.

William Blake

$\mathscr{E}$roticism is firstly a search for pleasure,

and the goal of techniques of love is to

attain the divine state, which is infinite

delight.

Kama Sutra

There is a duality of male and female in our powers and passions. We are, everyone of us, both male and female—active and receptive.

J. H. Noyes

An ancient hermetic teaching declares "as above so below." The person on top echoes the role of Heaven, whereas the one underneath corresponds to the Earth; either the male or female can fulfill these roles to complete satisfaction. Heaven and Earth "mutually complete each other."

Nik Douglas and
Penny Slinger

Opposites are of course likes, in reality; when things reach the limit of contrariety they come to resemble one another. This is decreed by God's omnipotent power, in a manner which baffles entirely the human imagination. Thus when ice is pressed a long time in the hand, it finally produces the same effect as fire. We find that extreme joy and extreme sorrow kill equally. Similarly with lovers: when they love each other with an equal ardor they will turn against one another without any valid reason, each purposely contradicting the other in whatever he may say; they quarrel violently over the smallest things, each picking up every word that the other lets fall and willfully misinterpreting it. All these devices are aimed at testing and proving what each is seeking in the other.

Ibn Hazm

*S*ex energy is the root of which love is the flower. It is the root of which sanctification is the flower. It is the root of which beauty is the flower. We cannot injure the root or reduce its vitality without injuring the flowers. It also furnishes the oil for the sacred lamp, and if the oil of joy is not available, the lamp will go out.

John S. Bayne

$\mathcal{A}$ total orgasm of the body and mind might be described as a showering of nectar from the head, running down your insides like a springtime shower. It is unmistakable, a wave of subtle chi energy that opens up hidden powers of feeling. You feel like a newborn baby, only adult and conscious.

Mantak Chia

$\mathcal{F}$eeling is everything.

Goethe

I slept, but my heart was awake. Hark! my beloved is knocking, saying, "Open to me, my love, my dove, my perfect one; for my head is wet with dew, my locks with the drops of the night. I had put off my garment, how could I put it on? I had bathed my feet, how could I soil them?" My beloved put his hand to the latch, and my heart was thrilled within me. I arose to open to my beloved, and my hands dripped with myrrh, my fingers with liquid myrrh, upon the handles of the bolt.

The Song of Solomon

Ah, sweet love long desired,

body gently made and narrow,

brightly colored face of youth,

that God formed with His hands!

In every time I have desired you,

for I have no pleasure in another thing,

I want no other love but the one.

                    Bernart de Ventadour

To love thee is the destiny inscribed on my forehead; the dust of thy threshold is my Paradise, thy radiant cheek my nature, to pleasure thee my repose.

Haféz

*M*ay your body never cease

to pay me attention,

may your love follow my face

as the cow follows her calf

from this day until my last.

Irish love charm

*F*or every man there is a woman worth

a thousand injuries.

Propertius

*S*he was a child, lifting her robe in the

garden,

There was no sin a lover of love could not

pardon;

It was as narrow as virtue, as easy as flying,

Yet I was halfway in when her petulent

sighing

Stopped me. I asked: "Why, why?" And she

said with a laugh:

"Moon of my eyes, I sigh for the other

half."

The Thousand and One Nights

*M*any mystical treatises point to the binding power of complementary breaths. One text states that "by meditating on the breath during lovemaking, one should seize the life-force of the other with the life-force of oneself, and bestow the life-force of oneself on that of the other." This is the Tantric love-pact which binds souls together throughout Eternity.

Nik Douglas and
Penny Slinger

I am as red and as beautiful as the
Rainbow.

I have just consumed your heart.

I have just consumed your blood.

I have just consumed your flesh.

I have just consumed your eyes.

I have just consumed your saliva.

Your saliva and mine are now one forever.

You are a magician!

Cherokee love song

Summer

Expansive, petulant, hot, and physical, love loves the body, and loves the experience of the body's very substance. Love is ardent and direct: a madness of intensity. Devotion becomes a palpable sense of the binding force of things. Devotion is in the very gesture of desire, and desire stands perfectly naked in the bright daylight of its purity, its naturalness, its ease, health, and rightness. All feeling flourishes in the senses, which is where everything takes place—all the comings and goings and workings of the world, wound into the hot circle of love's lusty, fiery embrace of self-transformation. Spirit partakes of the volatile nature of flesh and blood.

The time has come. The time has come.

The fever has come. Fire catches fire.

The fervor has come. Fire catches fire.

Fire heats the fiber round the pot. Then the
    whole house burns!

The time has come. I feel the fervor's come.

It's time to kill a vulture, and make your
    bush-bird live!

The time has come. Desire has come.

The time of the journey's come.

        Song of the Idoma tribe of Nigeria

First, if in her mind she desires to make love, then her breathing will become irregular. Second, if her Jade Gate desires to make love, then her nostrils will become distended and her mouth will open. Third, if her vital essence wishes to be stirred up through lovemaking, she will begin to move her body up and down rhythmically. Fourth, if her heart's desire is to be completely satisfied, then profuse moisture will be emitted from her Jade Gate, sufficient even to wet her clothes. Fifth, if she is ready to reach orgasm, she will stretch her body like an animal, and close her eyes.

Secret Methods of the Plain Girl

*S*he seizes him by the hair with one hand, and with the other takes him by the chin to lift him. She bites him wherever he had bitten her and rejoices at his effort to free himself. She embraces him with such force that their bodies become a single body.

Kama Sutra

$\mathcal{B}$ring your yo-yo, wind the string
  around my tongue,
Mama knows just how to make the yo-yo
  hum.
Bring your yo-yo, daddy, and we will have
  lots of fun.

                    Memphis Jug Band

When the body is naked, the life energies circulate more freely than when it is clothed.

Nik Douglas and
Penny Slinger

$\mathcal{R}$efrain from suppressing natural urges. Any suppression of our physical natures causes an inner reaction, a kind of distortion that destroys inner harmony. The whole range of physical, emotional and mental urges should be included in this admonition, even though such a statement may seem like an endorsement of self-indulgence. Self-indulgence is rarely the product of a natural urge.

Nik Douglas and
Penny Slinger

They (the harlots) smiled at him and approached him. As their rough breasts touched his lips, they pinned their fingers into his. They caressed and rubbed his face, neck and navel. They stretched their tongues on to his ears while saying, "These are the fresh blessings, receive them."

Bammera Potana

The bull-roarer talks.

The bull-roarer thunders.

"It has entered into me and become a child
in my womb.

My womb has opened at the sound of the
bull-roarer.

It has entered into me and become a child
in my womb.

I am in love."

The bull-roarer talks loud.

Aboriginal chant

Each sucks the passion from the other's lips, breathing lightly, lightly. In those willowy hips the passion beats; the mocking eyes, bright like stars. The tiny drops of sweat are like a hundred fragrant pearls; the sweet full breasts tremble. The dew, like a gentle stream, reaches the heart of the peony; and so they taste the joys of love in perfect harmony. For stolen joys, in truth, are even the most sweet.

Chin P'ing Mei

$\mathcal{L}$et me rest upon the image of your body! Stay close! You drive me crazy, you elate me, you take away from me too quickly the silent pleasure of pure contemplation. What majesty in these forms, what nobility in the inflections of this body! As beautiful as Ariadne sleeping!

Goethe

$\mathcal{A}$s long as life allows, let us fill our eyes with pleasure.

Propertius

They kiss the parts of the body of each other as though the moon is rotating around the earth. They intensify the love for each other by biting the cloth of each other with their teeth. The ocean of quality (Krishna) and the ocean of beauty (Radha) are indulged.

Surdas

Their high feast was love, who gilded all their joys. What better food could they have for body and soul? Man was there with Woman, Woman there with Man. What else could they be needing? They had what they were meant to have, they had matched the goal of their desire.

Tristan and Isolde

*M*ore happy love! more happy, happy
  love!
For ever warm and still to be enjoy'd,
For ever panting, and for ever young;
All breathing human passion far above,
That leaves a heart high-sorrowful and
  cloy'd
A burning forehead, and a parching tongue.

John Keats

By giving yourself to any beautiful sensation, however small, you more than double it—every time you touch good and enjoy it, you touch God; and there are infinite depths there, however small the surface may appear.

J. H. Noyes

Hither, hither, dear,
Be the breath of life
Hither, hither, dear!
Be the summer's wife!

Though one moment's pleasure
In one moment flies,
Though the passion's treasure
In one moment dies,

Yet it has not passed,
Think how near, how near!
And while it doth last,
Think how dear, how dear!

Hither, hither, hither,
Love this boon hath sent,
If I die and wither
I shall die content.

John Keats

*T*here is only one temple in the world,
and that is the human body. Nothing is
holier than this high form. One touches
heaven when one touches a human body.

Novalis

Her slender white neck, her chin,

mouth, brow, cheeks, and bright eyes are

the mirror of love, wherein one sees many

kinds of pleasure. If I could look into

that sweet mirror at every moment,

nothing better would ever happen to me.

Her neck, her eyes, her little breasts, chin,

cheeks, mouth—would that I could kiss

them secretly with her good will a hundred

thousand thousand times!

Ulrich von Lichtenstein

*W*hence originates these unions? They manifest through the earnest yearning and powerful drive that one tincture has for the other, which lies buried in the seeds of the temporal and outward nature. For in the tincture of the man, and thus also in the tincture of the woman, is a strong magnetic or driving power, that the one seeks the other, so that they may become one flesh, one nature, indeed, in some measure also even one person.

John Pordage

*B*ackward she push'd him, as she would
   be thrust,
And governed him in strength, though not
   in lust.

So soon was she along as he was down,
Each leaning on their elbows and their hips.
Now doth she stroke his cheek, now doth
   he frown,
And gins to chide, but soon she stops his lips,
And kissing speaks, with lustful language
   broken,
"If thou wilt chide, thy lips shall never open."

He burns with bashful shame, she with

    her tears

Doth quench the maiden burning of his

    cheeks;

Then with her windy sighs and golden hairs

To fan and blow them dry again she seeks.

He saith she is immodest, blames her miss;

What follows more, she murthers with a kiss.

Even as an empty eagle, sharp by fast,

Tires with her beak on feathers, flesh, and

    bone,

Shaking her wings, devouring all in haste,

Till either gorge be stuff'd, or prey be gone;

Even so she kiss'd his brow, his cheek, his
  chin,

And where she ends, she doth anew begin.

Forc'd to content, but never to obey,

Panting he lies, and breatheth in her face.

She feedeth on the steam, as on a prey,

And calls it heavenly moisture, air of grace,

Wishing her cheeks were gardens full of
  flowers,

So they were dew'd with such distilling
  showers.

William Shakespeare

*S*hove it in gently but enter deep

Then move it real slow

Move it slowly, slowly,

So that her body is not harmed.

Ancient Lett song

*T*he world is sexuality in action and there
is no escape from it. Sexuality contains the
germ both of the terrestrial man and of the
being which transcends humanity.

Trailok Chandra Majupuria

They looked upon each other, and their eyes

Gleam in the moon light; and her white arm clasps

Round Juan's head, and his around her's lies

Half buried in the tresses which it grasps:

She sits upon his knee, and drinks his sighs,

He, hers, until they end in broken gasps;

And thus they form a group that's quite antique,

Half naked, loving, natural, and Greek.

And when the deep and burning moments

    pass'd,

And Juan sank to sleep within her arms,

She slept not, but all tenderly, though fast,

Sustained his head upon her bosom's charms:

And now and then her eye to heaven is cast,

And then on the pale cheek her breast now

    warms,

Pillow'd on her o'erflowing heart, which pants

With all it granted, and with all it grants.

Lord Byron

*O*h to be naked like that, seeking joy
and peace of mind, facing the glorious part
of one's companion, both of us free to
murmur and sob?

Arthur Rimbaud

*O*nly by satisfying the need for physical
love will it be possible to guarantee the
development of the noble element in love.

Charles Fourier

$\mathcal{S}$ee how Radha and Krishna are sporting in love. He does not get happiness by merely embracing her. So he takes her into his arms for several times. The fiery sighs which are released from his mouth are drying the sweat drops on her body. No sooner the old sweat drops are dried up, the fresh drops appear over her body. He takes (the image of) his lover and places it in his eyelids.

Surdas

$\mathcal{S}$ex is the greatest thing in life. It cannot be left out of account. We ourselves are but expressions of it.

John S. Bayne

$\mathcal{E}$ssentially, orgiastic practices entail the reinvigoration of the same divine powers that inform all of nature.

Arthur Versluis

$\mathscr{I}$ urge you to come faster than the wind

to mount my breast and firmly dig and

plough my body, and don't let go until

you've flushed me thrice.

Classical Arab poem

*O*ne arousal and the ears and eyes are
sharp and bright.

Two arousals and the voice becomes clear.

Three arousals and the skin becomes radiant.

Four arousals and the backbone becomes
strong.

Five arousals and the buttocks become
muscular.

Six arousals and the "water course" flows.

Seven arousals and one becomes stout and
strong.

Eight arousals and the will is magnified and
expanded.

Nine arousals and one follows the glory of
heaven.
Ten arousals and one manifests spiritual
illumination.

Chinese sexual yoga classic

*L*ord, love me hard, love me long and
often. I call you, burning with desire. Your
burning love enflames me constantly. I am
but a naked soul, and you, inside it, are a
richly adorned guest.

Mechtild of Magdeburg

*N*ot from bamboo or stone, not played

    on strings,

This is the song of an instrument that lives,

That makes the emerald tassels quiver.

Who can say what the tune is, or the key?

The red lips open wide,

The slender fingers play their part daintily.

Deep in, deep out; the hearts grow wild with

    passion.

There are no words to tell of the ecstasy that

    thrills.

The Golden Lotus

*S*exual intercourse is in its nature the most perfect method of "laying on of hands" and under proper circumstances may be the most powerful external agency of communicating life to the body, and even the spirit of God to the mind and heart.

J. H. Noyes

*I*t is only when the phallus, the giver of semen, is surrounded by the yoni that God can manifest and the universe appear.

Alain Daniélou

Sexual gratification culminates in full orgasm of both partners with the friendliness and mutual feeling of intimacy that always results from the complete abandonment of self-assertiveness; where virile pride and femine passivity are thrown overboard without any attempt to do so.

Moshe Feldenkrais

Their two hearts beat as one,
They pressed together fragrant shoulders
And touched each other's cheeks.
He grasped that perfumed breast,
Smooth as the softest down,
And found it perfect.

Chin P'ing Mei

He bartered my heart,

looted my flesh,

claimed as tribute

my pleasure, took over

all of me.

> Mahadeviyaka

Mating is a secret code language in

which messages of great worth and moment

are recorded.

> Trailok Chandra Majupuria

$\mathcal{O}$ne might quite properly speak of a condensed recapitulation of sexual development as taking place in each individual sex act. It is as though the individual erotogenic zones were smouldering fires connected by a fuse which finally sets off the explosion of the charge of instinctual energy accumulated in the genital.

Sandor Ferenczi

The meaning of love, its idea and principle, is victory over the fallen life of sex. Love must conquer the old matter of sex and reveal the new, in which the union of man and woman will mean not the loss but the realization of virginity, i.e., of wholeness. It is only from this fiery point that the transfiguration of the world can begin.

Nicholas Berdyayev

When both are locked in the embrace
    of love,
There is no separateness, no "good" or "bad";
All thoughts vanish
With the onslaught of pure passion.

Kuttani Mahatmyam

Two youngsters had the itch,

Two youngsters in the ditch.

Horses came, and they were rich.

Two youngsters scratched their itch,

They galloped off at fever pitch,

And yet they never left the ditch!

No, they never left the ditch.

Song of the Idoma tribe of Nigeria

*W*hatever the circumstances, open or secret kisses cause both man and woman wonderful pleasure. When lovers kiss, their purpose is to draw close to each other, to develop love and mutual trust. Kisses, quarrels, blows, scratches, and bites arouse amorous ardor and pleasure.

Kama Sutra

Drink at his mouth,
Forgetting the full red cups and reeling
    bowls.

Drink at his eyes,
Forgetting the purple scent of the vine.

Drink at his cheeks,
Forgetting the life of roses poured in crystal.

Drink at his heart,
Forgetting everything.

The Thousand and One Nights

His mouth half open uttering amorous
noises, vague and delirious, drank of the
face of that deer-eyed woman whose body
lay helpless, released of excessive delight,
the thrilling delight of embraces.

Jayadev

$\mathcal{M}$an was made subject to woman's charms in order that he might be charmed continually. Her charms were intended to be irresistible, but the delicacy of the human mechanism led to a misconception on man's part as to its true purpose and woman saw no way out of the dilemma. This purpose was not the ease that comes from [sexual physical] exhaustion, but the fulfillment of themselves through the creative expression and stimulation of the higher powers latent within them.

John S. Bayne

*F*ull nakedness! All joys are due to thee,

As souls unbodied, bodies unclothed must be,

To taste whole joys.

Then since that I may know,

As liberally as to a midwife, show

Thyself: cast all, yea, this white linen hence,

There is no penance due to innocence.

To teach thee, I am naked first; why then

What need'st thou have more covering than

a man?

John Donne

Clothed in joy and love,

She is seduction, grace and sex-appeal.

Honey-sweet are her lips, life is her mouth;

Adorned in laughing femininity.

> Babylonian-Akkadian love poem

*N*ow therefore, while the youthful hew

Sits on thy skin like morning glew,

And while thy willing Soul transpires

At every pore with instant Fires,

Now let us sport us while we may;

And now, like am'rous birds of prey,

Rather at once our Time devour,

Than languish in his slow-chapt pow'r.

Let us roll all our Strength, and all

Our sweetness, up into one Ball:

And tear our Pleasures with rough strife,

Thorough the Iron gates of Life.

Thus, though we cannot make our Sun

Stand still, yet we will make him run.

Andrew Marvell

*M*y soul is bound

By the scents of her body,

Jasmine and musk

And rose of her body,

Amber and nard,

The scents of her body.

The Thousand and One Nights

$\mathcal{T}$he only way to feed on beauty is to feast one's eyes upon it; and to man, beauty is a real and essential food. It is a food which is assimilated in his body and essential to his life, without which he cannot live and be himself.

John S. Bayne

The bath hall was scented with the smoke of aloes and filled with expert girls, who undressed me and gave me a bath which made me lighter than a bird. When they had scented me and attired me richly, though slightly, they left me at the door of a private chamber where my naked bride awaited me.

She came to me and took me, tumbled me beneath her and rubbed me with astonishing passion, until all my soul rushed into a part of me which you can divine, my lord. I set to the work required of me, the work under my hand; I reduced that which there was to reduce, I broke that which there was to break, and ravished that which there was to ravish. I took what I might, I gave what I ought; I rose, I stretched, I drove in, I broke up, I plunged, I forced, I stuffed, I primed, I sank, I teased, I ground, I fell, and I went on again. I swear, O King of time, that my rascal earned his names of ram, smith, stunner, sweet calamity, long one, iron, weeper, workman, horner, rubber, old irresistible, staff, prodigious tool, pathfinder, blind fighter, young sword, great swimmer, nightingale, thick-neck father, father of nerves, him of the large eggs, old man with a turban, bald head, father of thrusts, father of delights, father of terrors, cock of the silence, daddy's little one, the poor man's wealth, old muscle of caprice, and mighty sugar-stick. I gave a separate example for each name and only made an end in time for the morning prayer.

We lived together thus in a sweet drunkenness.

The Thousand and One Nights

Of that which man holds dear, nothing exceeds the desires of the bedroom.

Chinese sexual yoga classic

*M*y beloved, man of my choice,

May you put your right hand in my vulva,

With your left stretched towards my head,

When you have neared your mouth to my

    mouth,

When you have taken my lips into your

    mouth,

Thus you swear the oath to me.

                 Sumerian hymn

*N*ow in more subtle wreaths I will entwine

My sinewy thighs, my arms and legs with

thine;

Thou like a sea of milk shalt lie displayed,

Whilst I the smooth, calm Ocean invade

With such a tempest as when Jove of old

Fell down on Danae in a storm of gold.

Yet my tall pine shall in the Cyprian strait

Ride safe at anchor and unlade her freight;

My rudder with thy bold hand like a tried

And skillful pilot thou shalt steer, and guide

My bark into love's channel, where it shall

Dance as the bounding waves do rise or fall.

Then shall thy circling arms embrace and clip

My naked body, and thy balmy lip

Bathe me in juice of kisses, whose perfume

Like a religious incense shall consume

And send up holy vapors to those powers

That bless our loves and crown our sportful

    hours.

Thomas Carew

Naked was she to all of my worship,

Triumphantly smiling from the heights of
her couch

At my love's desire advancing toward her,
as gentle and deep

As the sea sending its waves onto the dunes.

Charles Baudelaire

*T*he languishing eye

Puts in connection soul with soul,

And the tender kiss

Takes the message from member to vulva.

The Perfumed Garden

*T*here has never been any forbidden

fruit. Only temptation is divine.

André Breton

He's the kind of man that I want
around,
Handsome and tall and a teasing brown,
He's got to wake me every morning 'bout
half past three,
Kick up my furnace and turn on my heat,
Churn up my milk, cream my wheat,
Brown my biscuits, and chop my meat,
He's long and tall, and that ain't all,
He's got to be just like a cannonball,
That's why I want him around,
'Cause I'm the hottest gal in town.

Lil Johnson

$\mathcal{F}$ew penises sleep so soundly they cannot
be awakened with a kiss—but this kiss is not
the peck of a bird, it is the tongue, palate, and
lips of a hungry calf noisily sucking at a teat.

Geisha saying

$\mathcal{S}$weet breezes coming from over yonder
where my beloved lies sleeping, bring me
the libation of his sweet breath! My mouth
opens from my great desire to have it.

Raimbaud de Vaqueyras

He strokes my back, my stomach, my
   sides,

Kisses my cheeks, and anon begins to suck
   at my lips.

He embraces me close, and makes me roll
   on the bed,

Every part of my body receives in turn his
   love-bites,

And he covers me with kisses of fire.

The Perfumed Garden

$\mathcal{G}$o with it with a will, my dears,

This is no time for fears;

God made one picture better far

Than painter's pictures are:

A naked boy and girl in bed,

His arm holding her head,

His face bent forward on her breast,

And all the tinted rest:

Wishing this picture to be duplicated

And all the young world mated.

The Thousand and One Nights

*E*ros, blind father, let me show you the
way.
I beg of your all-powerful hands
his sublime body poured in flame
over my body fainted in roses!

Delmira Agustini

*T*ogether, facing each other, let us make
the stuff of realization!

Li Ho

She sinketh down, still lingering
on his knecke,
He on her belly falls, she on her backe.
Now is she in the verie lists of love,
Her champion mounted for the hot
encounter,
All is imaginarie she doth prove,
He will not manage her, although
he mount her.

William Shakespeare

The night thickened around us like a
    dividing wall,
And my eyes sensed yours in the darkness,
And I drank your breath, O ambrosia!
    O poison!
And your feet fell asleep in my fraternal
    hands.

The night thickened around us like a
    dividing wall.
I know the art of evoking happy moments,
And relive my past pressed tightly to your
    knees.

For what good would it be to seek your
    languid beauties
Save in your beloved body and your tender
    heart?

Charles Baudelaire

*M*y loved one came
Like a breeze from the south,
Shoulder to shoulder,
Mouth to mouth.

18th-century Irish lyric

*M*usk kisses,

To faint under musk,

To feel his body bend like a wet branch

That has eaten of the west wind and drunk

dew.

Musk kisses,

Beauty looked into his mirror at morning

And turned from her own shadow

To love the musk, musk, musk of his

nakedness.

The Thousand and One Nights

*O*ur breath shall intermix, our bosoms
   bound,
And our veins beat together; and our lips
With other eloquence than words, eclipse
The soul that burns between them, and the
   wells
Which boil our being's inmost cells,
The fountains of our deepest life, shall be
Confused in Passion's golden purity.

Percy Bysshe Shelley

Hear the sound of their buttocks, the men
moving their penises
For these beautiful girls, of the western tribes
And the penis becomes erect, as their buttocks
move
They are always there at the place of Standing
Clouds, of the Rising western clouds,
Pushed on to their backs, lying down among
the cabbage palm foliage.

Semen flowing from them into the young girls
For they are always there, moving their
buttocks.

They are always there at the wide expanse of

    water

Ejaculating among the cabbage palm foliage.

              Aboriginal erotic song cycle

*B*eing and nirvana—tabor and drum.

Mind and breath—rattle and cymbal.

Hail! Hail! The drum is sounded!

Whoever is devoted to the Gypsy woman

Will not let go for a moment,

    intoxicated with naturalness.

                     Krishna

And one thing I forbid you
Very firmly above all others,
Never should you name that (no)thing
that these men dangle around with them.

My good mother, is it then a ladle
Of a diving bird who knows how to plunge
And how swim in my father's
Pond and brook?

Good daughter, I will say it to you,
Yes, and by the faith that you owe me
Let it be a forbidden term
And let rectitude and reason say it,
I am telling you here that it is a prick.

Prick, she said, thank God a prick
Prick I'll say, whomever it bothers
Prick, you wretched woman! My father said
    prick,
My sister said prick, prick said my brother
And our chambermaid said prick,
A prick in front and a prick behind
Everyone calls it that at his will.

In truth, mother, you yourself
Say prick, and miserable me
What crime have I committed that I not
    call it a prick?
God grant me a prick so that I won't be
    lacking.

*(Shortly afterwards, Robert, aware of the
prohibition that her mother cast on the word,
approaches the daughter in a state of erection.)*

Hail, Robert! May God bless you!
Tell me, and may God assist you,
What you are holding. And he said to her:
My lady, this is a squirrel:
do you want it?

Medieval fabliau lyric

*T*he organs of sex and the natural laws
that govern them witness and always have
witnessed to the truth.

John S. Bayne

*I*t is ten times more pleasant to make
love during the day than at night. The
particular attraction lies in being able to
behold the other's nakedness, for such a sight
increases the desire.

Jou Pu Tuan

*O*ne day when Coyote was walking through Snoqualmie Pass, he met a young woman.

"What do you have in your pack?" she said.

"Fish eggs."

"Can I have some?"

"If you close your eyes and hold up your dress."

The woman did as she was told.

"Higher. Hold your dress over your head."

Then Coyote stepped out of his trousers and walked up to the woman.

"Stand still so I can reach the place."

"I can't, there's something crawling between my legs."

"Keep your dress up. It's bumble bee. I'll get it."

The woman dropped her dress.

"You weren't fast enough. It stung me."

Native American (Skagit) poem

*P*ressing breasts together and entwining
thighs moves her heart.

Leaning together and embracing shoulders,
the true pleasure is near.

These are the wondrous tidings of the
strummed zither.

No need to pluck with fingers to produce
the pure sound.

Chinese sexual yoga classic

And when is it that man is called one? When man and woman are joined together sexually. Come and see! At the point at which a human being as male and female is united, taking care that his thoughts are holy, he is perfect and stainless and is called one. Man should therefore act so that woman is glad at that moment and has one single wish together with him, and both of them united should bring their mind to that thing. For thus has it been taught, "He who has not taken a woman is as if he were only a half."

The Zohar

$\mathcal{V}$enus loves Mars, because Beauty,
which we call Venus, cannot subsist without
contrariety.

Pico della Mirandola

$\mathcal{L}$ook how my lovely has made me
whisper. When it comes to love, no one is
loyal anymore. A beautiful woman is desired
by each for himself. Kinsmen, friends,
everyone is contaminated and stirred up
by this god.

Propertius

$\mathcal{L}$ove is in truth a baffling ailment,
it is a delightful malady, a most desirable
sickness. Whoever is free of it likes not
to be immune, and whoever is struck down
by it yearns not to recover.

Ibn Hazm

*B*efore making love, in order to stimu-
late desire, the woman should behave just as
the man. Whatever the man practices on
the woman should also be practiced on him
by her.

Kama Sutra

$\mathcal{T}$he subtle center situated at the base of the spine is a triangle of desire, knowledge, and action, which forms the womb at whose heart rises the phallus that is born of its own self, shining like a thousand suns.

Shiva Purana

She made the bedstead ready, provided with the rarest luxuries, including a bronze censer for scenting the quilts. She let down the bed-curtains to the floor. The mattresses and coverlets were piled up, the pointed pillows lay across them. Then she shed her upper robe and took off her undergarment, revealing her white body, with thin bones and soft flesh. When then we made love with each other her body was soft and moist like ointment.

Mei-jen-fu

$\mathcal{Y}$ou don't satisfy a girl with presents and flirting, unless knees bang against knees and his locks into hers with a flushing thrust.

Classical Arab poem

*S*he gently moves her slender hips;

He hastens to extend the Precious Scepter.

Then, with ears pressed close to listen,

They whisper sweet endearments of their love.

Chin P'ing Mei

*T*here is tremendous importance in the action of sexual passion. Governed by God, mixed with benevolence, sweetened by the spirit of heaven, it is productive of unbounded happiness and improvement.

J. H. Noyes

*S*he's all states, and all princes, I,

Nothing else is.

Princes do but play us; compared to this,

All honor's mimic; all wealth alchemy.

Thou, sun, art half as happy as we,

In that the world's contracted thus;

Thine age asks ease, and since thy duties be

To warm the world, that's done in warming us.

Shine here to us, and thou art everywhere;

This bed thy center is, these walls, thy

    sphere.

                    John Donne

*N*ow put your arms around me, mama,

    like the circle round the sun,

I want you to love me, mama,

    like my easy rider done.

             Memphis Jug Band

Although my partner's passion has become intense, I am oblivious. With trusting sincerity, she reveals her secret, as I wait for the right moment. When she lowers her head and closes her eyes, the true lead has arrived. Over long distance, it comes flying like racing fire.

Chinese sexual yoga classic

I never tried to make him

stay inside me,

the Lord came on his own

and stole away my heart,

he sticks to my flesh

and mixes with my breath of life—

when this is his way

could he ever let me go?

Nammalvar

The men sit close together.

There is a rainbow across the sky.

The men wear rainbow decorations across

their chests.

The women see the rainbows.

The water penis, the lightning, strikes!

The water penis, the lightning, stands up!

Through the ground, the water penis stands

up.

This penis, this erect penis, crashes into

the ground.

This penis stands up.

The rim of the penis stands up.

The rim of the penis stands up.

The water penis, the erect penis,

    the lightning, ejaculates!

It throws the semen about.

The lightning, the water penis, stands up.

It is erect.

                Aboriginal "love magic" chant

*S*uddenly he lunged and reached the innermost Citadel, for within the Gate of Womanhood there is a Citadel, like the heart of a flower, which if touched by the Conqueror, is infused with wonderful pleasure.

Chin P'ing Mei

*H*appiness consists of having many passions and many means of satisfying them.

Charles Fourier

Fall

Love raises up and looks around in awareness. Love stores up its desire and cherishes. Devotion is a bountiful harvest, a work of preparation and thankfulness. Our hearts are full, our love is complex and maturing. Paradise is a home; a place of shelter and rest. The torrential rivers of desire have calmed but still run true to the ocean's depths. The sacredness of sex is manifest as warmth and love and holding. Our embrace is the articulation of a prayer. What was ardent is now adoring and full of peace. Love returns to the heart and soul, and sex becomes reflective sacred ceremony.

Spears criss-cross

Against the light,

Making a trellis

That stands upright.

Out of darkness

Like stems of grass

Shoots that steel mesh.

Men and women's forces

Are those spears.

Out they start

At cross-purposes

As light appears.

But, as their courses

Intersect, they knit

Into a net.

Each stake in being

Was a dart;

Now, is a matching

Counter-part

Of the cross-hatching.

> Song of the Idoma tribe of Nigeria

You say you love, but with a voice

Chaster than a nun's, who singeth

The soft Vespers to herself

While the chime-bell ringeth—

Oh, love me truly!

Oh, breathe a word or two of fire!

Smile as if those words should burn me,

Squeeze as lovers do—oh, kiss

And in thy heart inurn me!

Oh, love me truly!

John Keats

I wonder by my troth, what thou, and I
Did, till we lov'd? were we not wean'd till
　　then?
But suck'd on countrey pleasures, childishly?
Or snorted we in the seaven sleepers den?
T'was so; But this, all pleasures fancies bee.
If ever any beauty I did see,
Which I desir'd, and got, t'was but a dreame
　　of thee.

John Donne

*H*appiness both given and received is mutual enjoyment. For this shared happiness and pleasure, a man is willing to give himself entirely. For a man as well as a woman, the total gift of self is a source of wonderful happiness and luck. Sexual intercourse is not merely a pleasure of the senses: more importantly it is the sacrifice of oneself, the gift of self. To understand the mystery of sexual intercourse, to know and make use of what is fitting is the essential difference between man and beast.

Kama Sutra

*W*hat is all that men have done and
thought over thousands of years, compared
to one moment of love?

Friedrich Holderlin

*T*he accumulated force of sex energy
represents the world's great reservoir of virile
life, and if it is not generated, or being
generated, is dissipated, death is the inevi-
table consequence.

John S. Bayne

All fellowship is of the nature of sexual intercourse.

J. H. Noyes

He who is brought up in softness and ease cannot travel to the beloved. To make love is the joy of the adventurers.

Haféz

He wrestled seven bulls,

swallowed seven worlds,

filled me with the coolness of his heaven

and became my very mind.

O breath

that gives life to my flesh,

what a treasure you are!

Because you are here within me

and I

have mingled our beings.

Nammalvar

O night that was my guide,

O night more friendly than the dawn!

O tender night that tied

lover and the loved one,

loved one in the lover fused as one!

On my flowering breasts

which I had saved for him alone,

he slept and I caressed

and fondled him with love,

as cedars fanned the air above.

Wind from the castle wall,

while my fingers played in his hair

its hand serenely fell

wounding my neck, and there

my senses vanished in the air

I lay. Forgot my being,

and on my love I leaned my face.

All ceased. I left my being,

leaving my cares to fade

among the lilies far away.

St. John of the Cross

*H*e who understands that every sexual act is a hymn addressed to Vama-deva, the fiery form of Siva, re-creates himself with each copulation. He will thrive all the days of his life; he will live long and become wealthy in both offspring and livestock; rich will be his renown.

Chandogya Upanishad

The act of love is a meditation on the great life force.

Mantak Chia

The transmission of the genetic code and its transplanting into a new being of an ancestral heritage containing the archetypes bequeathed by divine thought, is the most important religious act of a man's life. It must be practiced as a ritual, following rules that take into account the most favorable moments, and the convergence of the stars.

Alain Daniélou

I'm goin' to get deep down in this

connection,

keep on tangling with your wire,

I'm goin' to get deep down in this connection,

umm keep tangling with your wire,

And when I mash down on your starter,

your spark plug will give me power.

Robert Johnson

*E*very time a man wishes to make love, there is a certain order of things to be followed. In the first place the man should harmonize his mood with that of the woman. Only then will his jade stalk rise.

Su-nu-ching

*T*here is no mystery to the Tao of intercourse. It is simply to be free and unhurried and to value harmony above all.

Chinese sexual yoga classic

*T*he rituals that provide the means for us to communicate with the gods are interwoven with the act of making love.

The first appeal is the invocation of the god *(hinkara)*.

The invitation represents the laudes *(prastara)*.

Sleeping next to the woman is the magnificat *(udgitha)*.

Facing one another is the choir *(pratihara)*.

The orgasm is the consecration.

Separation is the closing hymn *(nidhana)*.

Chandogya Upanishad

What then is the method of those who
pursue love, and what is the conduct which
with its eagerly straining zeal is to be called
love? What actually is this striving? It's the
use of both body and soul to mate with a
beautiful object and beget something on it.
And so when that which is pregnant with
the desire to beget approaches the beautiful,
it grows not only gracious, it is so joyously
excited that it flows over with its impulses
of mating and begetting. For love is not
love of the beautiful, it is engendering and
begetting upon the beautiful.

Plato
(spoken by Diotima)

*U*npin that spangled breastplate which
   you wear
That th' eyes of busy fools may be stopped
   there.
Unlace yourself, for that harmonious chime
Tells me from you that now it is bed-time.
Off with that happy busk, which I envy,
That it still can be and still can stand so
   nigh.
Your gown going off, such beauteous state
   reveals
As when from flowery meads th' hill's
   shadow steals.

Off with that wiry cornet and show

The hairy diadem which on you doth grow:

Now off with those shoes, and then safely

   tread

In this love's hallowed temple, this soft bed.

John Donne

*S*he tosses in her sleep and rolls over

the whole width of the bed. She turns away

from me, but leaves my hand in hers.

It is enough to press her hand to see her

heavenly eyes anew.

Goethe

*T*hough a woman is naturally reserved

and keeps her feelings concealed, yet when

she gets on top of a man she should show all

her love and desire.

Kama Sutra

$\mathcal{F}$ull orgasm accompanied by intense gratification is a physiological necessity. It is as important as procreation. From the standpoint of functioning of the individual frame, it even takes precedence over procreation. No matter how varied one's life may otherwise be, without the occasional absolute abandonment of the protective and self-assertive habits—as occurs only in frank, spontaneous, and harmonious relationship between man and woman—there always remains an anxious longing for something sensed as an ideal state of peaceful well-being.

Moshe Feldenkrais

Shedding my robes and removing my
makeup,
I roll out the picture-scroll by the pillow's
side;
Acting as an Initiatress into the Arts of
Love,
We perfect the postures and taste those rare
delights.

Chang Heng

Tyrannously I crave, I crave alone,

Her splendid body, Earth's most eloquent

Music, divinest human harmony;

Her body now a silent instrument,

That 'neath my touch shall wake and make
    for me

The strains I have but dreamed of, never
    known.

Arthur Symons

Since nature's first thrust is always toward the physical, it would be contrary to the natural order of things to begin by occupying lovers with transcendent and spiritual illusions. The natural impulses should first be reinforced and then the sentiments should be brought into play. When sentimental inclinations are linked to the physical ties already established, pleasure will be compounded.

Charles Fourier

$\mathcal{B}$e devoted to everything you believe in and especially the transforming power of sexual energy.

Nik Douglas and
Penny Slinger

$\mathcal{I}$t is the duty of the man to consider the tastes of woman and to be tough or tender, according to his beloved's wishes.

Koka Shastra

There are no lower passions. We require
a new conception of the sanctity of these
things. What we have despised and dishon-
ored are sacred things, and they must be
restored to the honor which is their due.

John S. Bayne

You got Jordan River in your hips,
mama,
Daddy's screaming to be baptized.

J. D. Short

$\mathcal{N}$ature has made union between the sexes the condition of our existence and the perpetuation of our species; in addition to this perpetuation, it has attached the most potent power of attraction and the most intense voluptuousness to this union: why then do we conceal it like an infraction or a crime? Why do we label as shameful those sexual organs upon which nature has concentrated all her industry and blush to reveal what should be a source of pride?

Alcide Bonneau

*B*ut how to reach that point of tenderness, where both lovers joyously yield and receive life from one another? First understand [that] the principle of polarity is dominant in sexual practice. Yin and yang energies are not separate energies: they are one and the same energy, but with two different charges. They never exist apart from one another, but are always in fluid motion. That is how man and woman can become "one": they simply realize the flow of sexual energy between them is continuous and belongs to them both.

Mantak Chia

$\mathcal{I}$ prefer over constancy, opium,

and nights

The elixir from your lips where love

flaunts itself;

When the caravan of my desires sets off

toward you,

Your eyes are the oases where my cares

may drink.

Charles Baudelaire

Spiritual longing attracts ecstasy and fills
life with lasting meaning.

Nik Douglas and
Penny Slinger

After my body became
One with yours, who could I serve?
After my mind became
One with yours, who could I summon?
Once my awareness was lost in Thee,
Who could I know?

Akka Mahdevi

Sexual desire is like a running stream and
the stream of man and woman join and flow
together spontaneously. Desire is a pure
thing like sunshine or fire or rain.

Trailok Chandra Majupuria

*M*y honey of the mother who gave birth
to her
My juicy grape, my honey sweet, my her-
mother's honey-mouth,
The glance of your eye delights me, come,
beloved sister,
The words of your mouth delight me, come,
my beloved sister,
Kissing your lips delights me, come, beloved
sister!
O my sister, the beer of your grain is delicious, come, my beloved sister!

In your house, your passion, come, my

    beloved sister

Your house is a storehouse, my her-mother's

    honey-mouth.

Sumerian hymn

*L*ike a great storm

the two of us shake

the tree of life

down to the most hidden

fibers of its roots.

Pablo Neruda

My friend is ocean to this river,

my friend is the shore to this shoreless river.

The current bends again.

At one such bending he will call to me,

and I will look upon his face,

and he will catch me up in his embrace,

and then my flame, my pain, will be

    extinguished.

And on his breast will be extinguished,

    in my joy, my flame.

Baul Gangaram

$\mathcal{L}$ove, loving, the friend and the beloved
are so directly united in the beloved that
they are in essence one presence, and the
friend and the beloved are, at the same time,
distinct, concordant, with no contradiction
or diversity of essence.

Ramon Llull

Bless those wonderful nights, and best of all Saturdays. If you had been there you'd have seen us locked together under the chaperone's sleepful eyes like the sun in the arms of the moon or a panting gazelle in the clasp of a lion.

Classical Arab poem

There is no sophism more deadly than the one that consists in presenting the accomplishment of the sexual act as being necessarily accompanied by a falling-off of amorous potential between two beings, a falling-off which, repeating, would lead them progressively to no longer suffice for each other. In that way, love would lay itself open to ruin, to the very extent to which it pursued its own realization. So Juliet, continuing to live, would no longer always be *more* Juliet for Romeo!

André Breton

A long, long kiss, a kiss of youth and
     love,
And beauty, all concentrating like rays
Into one focus, kindled from above;
Such kisses as belong to early days,
Where heart, and soul, and sense in concert
     move,
And the blood's lava, and the pulse a blaze,
Each kiss a heart-quake,—for a kiss's
     strength,
I think it must be reckoned by its length.

                                    Lord Byron

I kiss your mouth. Ah, love,

Could I but seal its ruddy, shining spring

Of passion, parch it up, destroy, remove

Its softly-stirring crimson welling-up

Of kisses! Oh, help me, God! Here at

   the source

I'd lie for ever drinking and drawing in

Your fountains, as heaven drinks from

   out their course

The floods.

D. H. Lawrence

When energies are exchanged and channeled through Tantric love-postures, they cause a resonance that travels beyond the dimensions of our world. Several Tantric texts refer to sexual postures as vehicles for superhuman or out of the body travel.

Nik Douglas and
Penny Slinger

*P*leasure, in the Shaivite conception, is an image of the divine state. This is why when the divine manifests itself in its procreative aspect, it shows its aspect as pleasure in equal degree. The sexual organ therefore has a double role: the inferior one of procreation, and the superior one of contacting the divine state by means of the ecstasy caused by pleasure *(ananda)*.

Alain Daniélou

*K*rishna brought his lady-love to his chest. The pleasure which is derived after touching the breasts with the chest cannot be properly explained. Krishna gazed at the limbs of Radha, which are of a golden color and which are smeared with the western-ghat sandals. Thinking that he is the lucki-est person on earth, he kisses her and takes her into his hands with happiness. They play the games of love. They keep their necks on the shoulders of each other. The red and the black cheeks shine with the nectars of lips. There are the impressions of kisses on the cheeks of both the lovers. They enjoy in the company of each other. They are one in two bodies.

Surdas

*T*o the most dear, to the most beautiful
Who fills my heart with brightness,
To the angel, to the immortal idol.

She diffuses through my life
Like air alive with brine,
And in my insatiated soul
Pours the flavor of eternity.

Charles Baudelaire

My heart and my arteries, and all my limbs quivered and trembled with desire. I felt myself so violently and dreadfully tested that it appeared if I did not give satisfaction to my lover entirely, to know him, to taste him in every part of his body and if he did not respond to my desire, I would die of rage. . . . He came, handsome and sweet, with his splendid face. I approached him submissively, like someone who belongs completely to another. And he gave himself to me as he usually does, in the form of the sacrament. Then he came in person to me and took me in his arms and locked me in his arms. All my limbs felt this contact with his with equal intensity, following my heart, as I had desired. Thus, externally, I was satisfied and quenched, following which, I remained merged with my lover until I had melted entirely within him in such a way that nothing was left of me.

Hedewijch

$\mathcal{P}$hysical love offers numerous opportunities to discover new things about oneself. As the singularly significant act that has the power to endow life, sexual love has a deep mystic meaning. If a couple can learn to use the power of sex creatively, they will discover mysteries beyond this world.

Nik Douglas and
Penny Slinger

I boast of my place with you

    I treasure my belief in you

Happiness overflowed for me

    I found it is not denied

I praise the luck that threw

    My lot with you and I increase.

Ibn Zaidun

I love and desire her with a heart so full, from excessive ardor, I think to be stealing her from myself, if one can lose something by loving it too well. For her heart submerges mine completely with a wave that does not evaporate.

Arnaut Daniel

When he sees me in heat he quickly
comes to me,
Then he opens my thighs and kisses my belly,
And puts his tool in my hand to make it
knock at my door.
Soon he is in the cave, and I feel pleasure
approaching.
He shakes me and trills me, and hotly we
both are working,
And he says, "Receive my seed!" and I
answer, "Oh, give it, beloved one!"
It shall be welcome to me, you light of my eyes!

The Perfumed Garden

Since everything about her is as
    balm to me,
There is nothing to be preferred.
When all delights me, I do not know if
One thing seduces me more than another.
She dazzles me like the Dawn
And consoles me like the Night
And the harmony that governs all her
    beautiful body
Is too exquisite
For impotent analysis to
Enumerate its many harmonies.
O mystic transformation

Of all my senses fused into one!

Her breath makes music.

Like her breath makes perfume!

Charles Baudelaire

*D*ear dark head, darling mine,

put your arm around me, soft and white;

your honey-mouth, your breath of thyme—

who could not love you tonight!

18th-century Irish lyric

The beating of your heart is joyful
music,
Rise and let me make love to you!
In your delicious lap,
The one for love-making,
Your passion is sweet,
Growing luxuriantly is your fruit.
My bed of incense is perfumed.
Enter, I have opened my thighs.

Babylonian-Akkadian bridal song

*T*remble, tremble, aspen leaf,

The wind makes you quiver.

That's how young lads quiver

Sleeping next to lasses.

Ancient Lett song

*W*hat is it men in women do require?

The lineaments of Gratified Desire.

What is it women in men do require?

The lineaments of Gratified Desire.

William Blake

And there

Full mid-between the champaign of your

breast

I place a great and burning seal of love

Like a dark rose, a mystery of rest

On the slow bubbling of your rhythmic

heart.

D. H. Lawrence

*T*ake me into your embrace

Let me sleep close beside you

Take me into your embrace

Let me sleep close beside you

Take me in, my light, take me in

And put me out before the dawn

Greek Rembetica song

$\mathcal{S}$leeper, the palm trees drink the breathless

noon,

A golden bee sucks at a fainting rose,

Your lips smile in their sleep. Oh, do not move.

Sleeper, oh, do not move the gilded gauze

Which lies about your gold, or you will scare

The sun's gold fire which leaps within your

crystal.

Sleeper, oh, do not move. Your breasts in sleep,

Allah, they dip and fall like waves at sea;

Your breasts are snow, I breathe them like

sea foam,

I taste them like white salt. They dip and fall.

Sleeper, they dip and fall. The smiling stream

stifles its laugh, the gold bee on the leaf

Dies of much love and rosy drunkenness,

My eyes burn the red grapes upon your breast.

Sleeper, oh, let them burn, let my heart's

   flower,

Fed on the rose and sandal of your flesh,

Burst like a poppy in this solitude,

In this cool silence.

The Thousand and One Nights

$\mathcal{T}$he consummation of love exists at both outer and inner levels. On the outside, in the realm of the sense organs, the play of love is brought about through the contact of the bodies and senses. On the inside, erotic play takes place in the Subtle Body, the mind and the spirit. Orgasm resolves the bipolarity of "outer" and "inner."

Nik Douglas and
Penny Slinger

$\mathcal{D}$o not torment me, woman, let us set our minds at one, and let us put our arms around each other.

Set your strawberry-coloured mouth against my mouth, O skin like foam; stretch your lime-white rounded arm about me.

Slender graceful girl, admit me to your bed, let us stretch our bodies side by side.

15th-century Irish poem

*C*ome, draw near!
that I may contemplate your figure.

Your legs so well formed
Your legs trace the slenderness of the okwele
    tree
Your face is calm and clear
Like the line of the horizon of a far-off
    forest

The small space that separates your two
    breasts
Is beautiful like the wake of a fish's fin,
The tips of your breasts shiver
As if you were soaked by the rain!

Your neck curves beautifully
Like a boa powerfully coiling high up an
   anthill,

Your neck is a young gazelle's
The folds of your neck
Are like the smooth trunk of a palm tree!

Your belly is supple and smooth like a
   tender stem of asparagus.

                              Mbosi (Congo) poem

I know by his scent

Before he reaches my hair

That the breeze has risen and dances upon

    the meadow.

If one could take love as one takes a lover

And rest his head between the breasts

And know Peace!

The Thousand and One Nights

She appeared in the distance, tall
As the lightning that brushes a high palm
    tree.
The soft noise of her supple legs
Is like the compact stir of bears bursting out.
The warm hue of her skin
Is like a night owl's plumage eager to enter
    the forest.
And then she reclines on the bed,
Compact like a willow basket filled with salt,
Her body so perfect she floats in the air!

                Mbosi (Congo) poem

Which of our passions bears some mark of the divine spirit? Can we find any trace of that spirit in our frenzies of ambition, in our perfidious administrative and commercial affairs, in the inconstancy of our friendships, in the discords of our families? No, greed, deceit, and envy betray the absence of divine spirit. But there is one passion which retains its original nobility, which keeps the divine fire burning in mortal men, which gives them a share in the attributes of the Deity. This passion is love.

Charles Fourier

$\mathcal{T}$he orgasm is a "divine sensation."
The ecstasy of pleasure can reveal divine
reality leading to detachment and spiritual
realization.

Alain Daniélou

$\mathcal{Y}$our beauty reached me in my hiding
Your bounty rose over me in my seclusion
The changes did not cease when they ran
To you as a pledge of love and passion
You are enough for me.

Ibn Zaidun

Fair, agreeable, good friend,

when will I have you in my power,

lie beside you for an evening,

and kiss you amorously?

Be sure I'd feel a strong desire

to have you in my husband's place

provided you had promised me

to do everything I wished.

La Comtessa de Dia

*W*e dressed each other

Hurrying to say farewell

In the depth of night.

Our drowsy thighs touched and we

Were caught in bed by the dawn.

                    Japanese Empress Eifuku

My love's a love that has grown for

more than a year

It is a sorrow whispered low

It is a stretch of strength beyond enduring

It reaches the ends of the earth

And the high vault of the sky

It is heart cleaving, heart breaking

It is combat with shadow

It is drowning in water

It is a race against the heavens

It is heroic encounter with the sea

It is love echoing and re-echoing

My love for her for whom I have given my

life and my love.

9th-century Irish poem

$\mathcal{I}$make seven circles, my love

For your good breaking.

I make the gray circle of bread

And the circle of ale

And I drive the butter round in a golden ring

And I dance when you fiddle

And I turn my face with the turning sun till

your feet come in from the field.

My lamp throws a circle of light,

Then you lie for an hour in the hot unbroken

circle of my arms.

George Mackay Brown

*O*h, you man of all man, who fillest me

    with pleasure.

Oh, you soul of my soul, go on with fresh

    vigor,

For you must not yet withdraw it from me;

    leave it there,

And this day will then be free of all sorrow.

The Perfumed Garden

How delicious an instrument is woman,
when artfully played upon; how capable is
she of producing the most exquisite harmonies, of executing the most complicated
variations of love, and of giving the most
Divine of erotic pleasures.

Ananga Ranga

*W*hen uniting the mouth with the Yoni,
try to meditate on yourself as drinking from
the fount of immortality, the inexhaustible
Source of Life. By giving the best, you
receive the most; the Yoni opens herself up
and reveals all her secrets.

Nik Douglas and
Penny Slinger

$\mathcal{P}$rocreation's rituals are described in the Tantras. They include adoration of the genitals as images of the divine principles poised to unite to accomplish the miracle.

Alain Daniélou

$\mathcal{D}$o not expect that avoiding sex is an answer; sex must be conquered, redeemed, understood. Ordinary sex must be transmuted, sanctified.

Thomas White

With his imagination the Lover formed and pictured his Beloved's countenance in bodily wise, and with his understanding he beautified It in spiritual things; and with his will he worshiped It in all creatures.

Ramon Llull

Since I have hemm'd thee here

Within the circuit of this ivory pale,

I'll be a park, and thou shalt be my deer:

Feed where thou wilt, on mountain, or in dale;

Graze on my lips, and if those hills be dry,

Stray lower, where the pleasant fountains lie.

William Shakespeare

Thou hast ravished my heart with one
of thine eyes,
With one chain of thy neck.
How much better is thy love than wine,
and the smell of thine ointments than
all spices.
Thy lips, O my spouse, drop as the honey-
comb: honey and milk are under thy
tongue.

The Song of Solomon

$\mathcal{T}$urn toward me your azure eyes that are
   rich with stars!
For the divine balm of one delightful glance,
I will lift the veils from love's most obscure
   pleasures,
And you shall drowse in endless dream!

Charles Baudelaire

*I*f I am able to say or do anything of worth it is to her my thanks are due, for she gave me the craft and talent that have made me a merry poet. All I do that is pleasing, including even the thoughts that rise from my heart, I owe to her beautiful body, full of grace.

Peire Vidal

$\mathcal{T}$he power of passion is the greatest power in the world. We all know this. In fact, we are so conscious of its power that we are afraid of it.

John S. Bayne

$\mathcal{T}$hose who ask when the madness of love will be over do not know what they are saying. A true passion knows no end.

Propertius

The prick has a beautiful body

Until the day it dies.

And when it passes away,

Its tip is moist with golden dew.

Ancient Lett song

There is nothing so sweet in the world

As a woman's cunt, you can be sure of it.

She carries the large urn

That is worth all of a castle's gold.

Gautier le Lou

When I am the honest thief of my lady, I do not consider my pain as bad. When in her home I nakedly embrace and caress her flanks, I know no emperor who may win greater worth or obtain more of *fin'amour*.

Bernard Marti

I have been sorely troubled
about a knight I had;
I want it known for all time
how exceedingly I loved him.
Now I see myself betrayed
because I didn't grant my love
to him; I've suffered much distress
from it, in bed and fully clothed.

I'd like to hold my knight

in my arms one evening naked,

for he'd be overjoyed

were I only serving as his pillow,

and he makes me more radiant

than floris his blanchaflor.

To him I grant my heart, my love,

my mind, my eyes, my life.

La Comtessa de Dia

*S*entiment, which is the noble side of love, will endow all social relations with a unique charm. How will sentimental love maintain this dominion? Through the fact that the physical impulses, far from being fettered, will be fully satisfied. Through the fact that the need for physical gratification will no longer be regarded as any more indecent than the appetites of the other senses, the love of feasts, concerts, perfumes, finery, etc.

Charles Fourier

*L*ove is to be inclined towards something wholeheartedly, then to sacrifice one's body, soul and wealth all for that, then to attain complete inward and outward conformity with it and, with all this, to regard oneself as deficient in one's love.

> Harith al-Muhasibi

*L*ove consists in regarding your own much as little, and your Beloved's little as much.

> Ba-Yazid Bistami

*I*s there anything else two beings can do, joined for the moment and forever in the communion of love, besides feel the depths of that mystery and remain silent? This is the point, the marvelous limit, where the Word breaks off, defeated, and the pure act triumphs. Beyond this threshold, no word sounds.

Pierre Mabille

When a man has love on his side, he
should not talk too much.

Propertius

When I spread longing and affection as
a scroll before my inward eye, my yearning
grows, and my comrade, desire, grows, too,
as if he would mount to the clouds!

Tristan and Isolde

The moon of maya, the moon of gold,

Has let her moon-charm take on hold

So I have become a lost

Dreamer: such Moon Magic cost

It burns a Fire deep within

    Oh—

I burn my nights and days therein.

Bengali Baul song

*P*assion resides in the woman's right side during the bright fortnight of the lunar month, from new moon to full. The reverse is the case during the dark fortnight. The shifting of passion is believed to take place by the action of light and darkness.

Ananga Ranga

*T*he young moon is upon your forehead, wide are your lotus eyes, you are the home of the attractiveness of a hundred million loves.

Tulsi Das

$\mathcal{T}$he erotic sentiment stimulates faith and leads to commitment. Eroticism can create the awareness of a timeless state of nonduality. The truly erotic experience is always timeless; the couple evoke faith in each other and awaken the nondual essence within.

Nik Douglas and
Penny Slinger

Winter

The fire hides within; the embrace protects. Devotion is strong and abiding, and the physically ardent has become spiritually intense. Sexuality becomes pure expression, a form of meditation. Love is strong, mature, and inward. The light that shines in the world is an inward light. Desire has contracted into its source and become a seed of hope. Sex is inner knowledge.

Take off your cloak and your hat

And your shoes, and draw up at my hearth

Where never woman sat.

I have made the fire up bright;

Let us leave the rest in the dark

And sit by firelight.

The wine is warm in the hearth;

The flickers come and go.

I will warm your limbs with kisses

Until they glow.

D. H. Lawrence

For I love him so with my whole heart,
that always, when I go between sleeping and
waking I have one guide with him together:
play and pleasure and joy and laughter.
The content I have in silence and peace
no creature knows, while he lies in my arms,
till he is transfigured.

Peire d'Alvernhe

*F*or it comes to pass that sometimes
through greatness of devotion, or great
wonder, or exceeding exultation, the mind
cannot possess itself in any way, and being
lifted up above itself, passes into ecstasy.
The human mind is raised above itself by
the greatness of its devotion, when it is
kindled with such fire of heavenly desire that
the flame of inner love flared up beyond
human bearing.

Richard of St. Victor

With love as bowl,

ardor as oil,

and a joyful mind as wick,

I swooned

and lit a blazing lamp of knowledge.

Pulattalvar

With his imagination, the Lover formed and pictured the countenance of his Beloved in bodily form, and with his understanding, he beautified it in spiritual things, and with his will he worshipped it in all creatures.

Ramon Llull

$\mathcal{S}$exual love is a passion which is peculiarly allied to religion, in which the devout heart, holding the body within the bounds of chaste control, rises into communication with God.

J. H. Noyes

$\mathcal{T}$he restoration of paradise is the real secret of the mysteries of love.

Arthur Versluis

*L*ove's mysteries traditionally are seen in a complete religious context. This is true in the ancient mysteries, in terms of marriage with a god; it is true in the Christian mysteries, when it is a matter of the wedding of the Bride and Bridegroom; and it is still true among the troubadors. When love is purely individualized—i.e., when it is divorced from its spiritual context and becomes carnal (what most moderns think of as romantic love)—it no longer serves as sacred eros. Love's mysteries are not merely enhanced by spiritual discipline culminating

in angelic revelation—this discipline is
central. Without this religious context,
love's mysteries can lead lovers to hell.

Arthur Versluis

*L*ove is a divine flame, the true spirit of
God, who is love. Is it not in the rapture of
love that man reaches toward the heavens
and identifies himself with God? Is there
any lover who does not deify his or her loved
one and who is not convinced that their
shared love is a divine happiness?

Charles Fourier

O living flame of love!
O living flame of love
how tenderly you wound
my soul in her profoundest care!

You are no longer shy
do it now, I ask you:
break the membrane of our sweet union.

O soothing cautery!
O wound that is a joy!
O gentle hand! O delicate touch
tasting of eternity
repaying every debt!
Killing, you turn my death to life!

O lamps of human fire
in deep transparency
the lowest caverns of the senses,
once shadowy and blind,
give warmth and light
and strange beauty to her beloved!

How lovingly and soft
you make my breasts recall
where you alone lie secretly:
and with your honeyed breath
replete with grace and glory,
how tenderly you make me love!

St. John of the Cross

To do away with the sexual relation
would be to blot out the very sun from
the heavens.

J. H. Noyes

To love, to love, to love,
To be more, to be still more!
To love through love,
To be luminous in light!

Jorge Guillén

$\mathcal{T}$he act of love is particularly momentous for a human being. It involves one's entire destiny. The energy of every act and thought is preserved. When you raise your sexual seed-essence to a high level of spiritual intention, it becomes light-essence, or light seed that illuminates your path through life and beyond.

Mantak Chia

*S*uch a thing befalls me when I am in her presence that I cannot describe it to the intellect. It seems to me that as I gaze at her there issues from her semblance a lady of such beauty that the mind cannot grasp it, and from this at once another is born of wondrous beauty out of which it seems that there issues a star which says: "Behold, your blessedness is before you."

Cavalcanti

*W*hether the friend and the beloved are
near or far is all one and the same, for their
love mingles as water mingles with wine.
They are linked as heat with light; they
agree and are united as essence and being.

Ramon Llull

*H*ow well I know that flowing spring,
  though it is night

the eternal fountain is unseen.
How well I know where she has been,
  though it is night.

I do not know her origin.
None. Yet in her all things begin,
  though it is night.

I know that nothing is so fair
and earth and firmament drink there,
  though it is night.

I know that none can wade inside
to find her bright bottomless tide,
    though it is night.

Her shining never has a blur;
I know that all light comes from her,
    though it is night.

I know her streams converge and swell
and nourish people, skies, and hell,
    though it is night.
The stream whose birth is in this source
I know has a gigantic force,
    though it is night.

The stream from but these two proceeds
yet neither one, I know, precedes,
    though it is night.

She calls on all mankind to start
to drink her water, though in dark,
    though it is night.

O living fountain that I crave
in bread of life I see her flame,
    though it is night.

St. John of the Cross

*B*orn of the first dualism of the distinction of Person and Nature, desire, the attraction of opposites is the supernatural eros. Linked to nature by desire, the Cosmic Person gives birth to innumerable worlds.

Karaptri

*W*hatever one loves, one finds everywhere, and everywhere sees resemblances and analogies to it. The greater one's love, the vaster and more meaningful is this analogous world. My beloved is the abbreviation of the universe, the universe an elongation, an extrapolation of my beloved.

Novalis

Said the Lover to his Beloved: "Thou art all, and through all, and in all, and with all. I would give Thee all of myself that I may have all of Thee, and Thou all of me." The Beloved answered: "Thou canst not have Me wholly unless thou art wholly Mine." And the Lover said: "Let me be wholly Thine and be Thou wholly mine." The Beloved answered: "If I am wholly Thine what part in Me will thy son have, thy brother, thy sister and thy father?" The lover replied: '"Thou O my Beloved, art so great Whole, that Thou canst abound, and yet be wholly of each one who gives himself wholly to Thee."

Ramon Llull

*B*eyond life, my love, always farther beyond, now ethereal, unique, upon a couch of stars, we populate the limitless night, we live without death, oh my beauty, an infinite night.

Weary of the world my head settles softly on a bluish breast. I sense only your blood now peopled with lights, with myriad stars, and kiss the soft pulse of the universe and touch your face with the sublime radiance of my cheek.

Oh sad, oh grave total night. Beloved, you lie perfect and I retrace you, embrace you.

Solitary world. Universal living of a body,

made into lights, you permit love beyond

the life of a man.

Vicente Aleixandre

*B*esides the wintry water

she and I built

a red bonfire

wearing away our lips

from kissing each other's souls,

throwing everything into the fire

burning up our life.

Pablo Neruda

*L*et one sensual

love be born,

and my body as full of lust,

for I want the longing for you more

than kissing someone else in my arms.

Bertran de Born

Beyond us,

on the frontiers of being and time,

a greater life beckons us.

Lie down here on the edge of so much foam,

of so much life that does not know and

surrenders:

you too belong to the night.

Stretch out, whiteness that breathes,

throb, oh portioned star,

cup, bread that tips the balance to the side

of the dawn,

pause of blood between this time and

another without measure.

Octavio Paz

I am no longer the man who would fear death. Something else is even harder to me than death itself, the fear of not having your love any more at the moment I die.

Propertius

$\mathcal{F}$rom love, for here

Do we begin and end, all grandeur comes,

All truth and beauty—from pervading love—

That gone, we are as dust.

William Wordsworth

*L*ove is from love, from love the ocean

of existence may be crossed

Love binds the whole creation, love yields

the highest ends,

But one vow of love provides the sweet

salvation of life,

The vow of love is truth.

Sur Das

*T*here is a direct relationship between the highest mental and psychic powers in mankind and the secretions of the sex glands.

> *Tibetan Book of the Great Liberation*

*T*he vibrations of sex were not intended to be an exceptional experience but a constant renewal force.

> John S. Bayne

With his head resting between her thighs, the Adept drinks deeply from the Source of Life. Above, the goddess causes his power to grow and transform into Buddha-fields within her mind. Below the Adept endows each Wave of Wisdom with his means. Each meditating on the transcendental experience of nonduality, the confluence of rivers swells and bursts its banks; there are no limitations anymore.

Chandamaharosana Tantra

The road of love is the road without
end, and in which there is no hope save to
abandon our souls.

Haféz

Love can deny nothing to love.

Andreas Capellanus

*L*ove, all alike, no season knows, nor
  clime,
Nor hours, days, months, which are the rags
  of time.

                              John Donne

*T*rue love never decreases, even after one
hundred years.

                              Kama Sutra

If you want to know how the old man fared with me, this is what went on. He lolled me the whole night through, and when dawn flashed his private lips thundered rainlessly and his key wilted in my lock.

Classical Arab poem

Women [Aborigines] are generally considered—and consider themselves to be—sexually attractive even at very advanced ages. In many tribes, younger boys feel it is prestigious to have a sexual liaison with an older woman. [Aboriginal] Men must earn the right to marriage and sexuality through self-development and spiritual awareness.

Robert Lawlor

*L*et us forget that time exists and cease to reckon the days of our loves! What are centuries compared to the moment when two beings thus divine and approach each other?

Friedrich Holderlin

Ah, if she will allow me to spend
nights with her in this way, I will live a
whole lifetime in a single year! And if she
grants me many, that will be an immortality.

Propertius

$\mathcal{S}$ex energy is extraordinarily versatile, and can be transformed into many different functions. This is one reason it is so nourishing to our spiritual being.

Mantak Chia

$\mathcal{A}$ccording to *Tantras*, sex or the blending of polarities into one, is the universal basis of all phenomena irrespective of dimension and magnitude.

Trailok Chandra Majupuria

The sex organ is that organ by which communication is established between man and the creative force, the manifestation of the divine being.

Alain Daniélou

The phallus is the primary sensorial organ of the soul, it creates man, it gives birth to the imagination, it unleashes the thinking faculty in the individual.

Paini

Semen is the light imprisoned in the body.

Trailok Chandra Majupuria

Desire is a string stretched between two complementary forces; the sound this string produces is life. To create this sound the string must be vibrated by a shock: this shock is eroticism, which signifies the magic of vitality expressed principally through the awakening of sexual prowess.

R. A. Schwaller de Lubicz

A man's attitude toward woman is a
direct reflection of his attitude toward life.

> Nik Douglas and
> Penny Slinger

*T*he grace of your bright palms
Poise of your silken feet
Pale knees the snows cannot equal
These were my heart's deep.

> 16th-century Irish lyric

I shall never go away from her in

my life, as long as I am all in one piece;

for when the heart of it is gone,

the straw stands a long time wavering.

And if she does not rush forth at once,

I shall not censure her for that,

as long as, sometime, she makes up for it

in full.

Bernart de Ventadour

$\mathcal{I}$ consider love as a conjunction between scattered parts of souls that have become divided in this physical universe, a union effected within the substance of their original sublime element.

Ibn Hazm

$\mathcal{S}$ ex is one of the nine reasons for reincarnation. The other eight are unimportant.

Henry Miller

There is a way to use every form of external enjoyment, as a method of worship between us and the divine.

J. H. Noyes

And the *Sahajiyas* consider that chastity, especially under extreme temptation, has the power to transform desire into love. Self-enforced separation, when union is easy, purifies desire by intensifying it.

Edward C. Dimock

Of all the sentiments, the only one I regard as being fully sacred is love. The very notion of the sacred flows so directly out of love that without it no idea of sacred is even conceivable.

Benjamin Péret

The part of the body in which the sexual organs are located was called the "sacrum" by our ancestors because they knew what it was all about. *Sacrum* comes from Middle English *sacren,* meaning to consecrate. And that in turn comes from a word out of Greek and Latin antiquity: *sacer,* meaning dedicated to God. Our own word *sacred* comes from the same root and means the same thing: holy, set aside for God's use, God's service, God's purpose. What the word *sacrum* says is simply that sex is sacred. If this one word were widely understood, the destiny of the whole race would be altered.

Thomas White

Of all things that make mankind prosper, none can be compared to sexual intercourse. It is modeled after Heaven and takes its form by Earth; it regulates Yin and rules Yang. Those who understand its significance can nurture their nature and prolong their years. But the foolish people who cannot understand its significance harm themselves and die before their time.

Taoist master Tung

$\mathcal{I}$t is considered undesirable, even

dangerous, for a woman to be sexually

frustrated or circumstantially cut off

from sexual activity. As the Aborigines

say, "It makes for bad Magic."

Robert Lawlor

The fulfillment of this earth's law is love,

So, brothers and sisters, let us practice love!

With love two can live happily in the

smallest of rooms

Without love even in a palace two cannot

live in peace.

O, the fulfillment of this earth's law is love!

So, brothers and sisters, let us practice love!

The fulfillment of this earth's law is love!

So, brothers and sisters, let us practice love!

Love is above the Law, and it is the Law

completely,

Without love there'll be no help of one

    another.

O, the fulfillment of this earth's law is love!

So, brothers and sisters, let us practice love!

                       African love poem

*T*he sexual act is not to be concealed or suppressed but exalted and glorified as this process is continuously repeated in the sacred marriage of the primal divine couple. The union of sexes ensures the eternity of life.

                       Trailok Chandra Majupuria

*T*he bliss-wave of ecstasy passes through four spiritual desire-realms, from physical contact to longing, high passion, and transcendence. In these four stages, the sentiment of love is developed and sublimed.

Nik Douglas and
Penny Slinger

*O*n the way to spiritual realization, the realization of desires is essential.

Kama Sutra

*W*e bear life,

so painful and so short,

only for that:

caress, nibble or kiss

on that divine bread

for which our blood is our wine.

Rubén Darío

Amid the gloom and travail of existence suddenly to behold a beautiful being, and as instantaneously to feel an overwhelming conviction that with that fair form for ever our destiny must be entwined; that there is no more joy than in her joy, no sorrow but when she grieves; that in her sigh of love, in her smile of fondness, hereafter is all bliss; to feel our flaunty ambition fade away like a shrivelled gourd before her vision; to feel fame a juggle and posterity a lie; and to be prepared at once, for this great object, to forfeit and fling away all former hopes, ties, schemes, views; to violate in her favor every duty of society; this is a lover, and this is love.

Benjamin Disraeli

A true lover is constantly and without intermission possessed by the thought of his beloved.

Andreas Capellanus

These are the signs of the *nayika:* she is of greatest beauty and her qualities are equal to her beauty. By *bhava* [involvement in emotions and situations] she will come, suddenly, and be joined with him. Her beauty will pass though his eyes into his heart, and when it has entered his heart it will attract his mind.

Edward C. Dimock

My face in thine eye, thine in mine
appeares,

And true plain hearts doe in the faces rest,

Where can we finde two better hemispheares

Without sharpe North, without declining
West?

What ever dyes, was not mixt equally;

If our two loves be one, or, thou and I

Love so alike, that none doe slacken, none
can die.

John Donne

*O*h, if you'd have me,

I would walk the world proudly,

I'd take you over the water

With no thought of a dowry,

I'd leave my friends and my own people,

I'd have no fear of drowning,

For you'd save me from the grave, love,

If you placed your arms around me.

18th-century Irish lyric

*Y*our head of long black hair (do you remember?), I caressed with my hand, so that your generous lips would not leave me. White as the kiss that transfixed me inside you was the tender atmosphere surrounding us. I felt I embraced my entire life in embracing you.

José Marti

*S*ex is one instinct of man which can still make us experience a kind of near-mystical ecstasy. Sex is more than a biological necessity for propagation of species: it is also a spiritual need and so it has more than one purpose to serve.

Trailok Chandra Majupuria

*W*hatever names two lovers take, when
they come together it will be like the touch
of matter and antimatter, the passing and
the consuming passion of our world.

William Irwin Thompson

*C*ome to my arms & never more
Depart; but dwell for ever here:
Create my spirit to thy love.

William Blake

This love, in a mortal body, whereof I then was full, was like the joy that a chaste man has at the very time when he is in actual love and in the very act with his mate; such extreme pleasantness was suffused over the whole of my body, and this for a long time, lasting all the interval of waking, especially just before I went off to sleep, and after sleeping.

Emanuel Swedenborg

*I*s this love real

Or am I dreaming?

It is impossible to say

When both the real and the dream

Exist without truly existing.

Ono no Komachi

*B*ecause no slave is present

I am the servant

As well as the captive of my Beloved.

She places me within her orchard,

She gives me not water

When I wish to drink,

She does not fill my body

With water from the goatskin

But comes looking for me as an amusement!

Chester Beatty Papyrus

*L*ord, I cannot dance without your lead

If you would I leap with abandon

You must sing the song.

Then shall I leap into love,

From love into knowing

From knowing into bliss

And from bliss beyond all human sensations.

There I would stay, yet desire to circle yet

higher.

Mechtild of Magdeburg

*T*hou demandest what is love? It is that powerful attraction towards all that we conceive, or fear, or hope beyond ourselves, when we find within our own thoughts the chasm of an insufficient void, and seek to awaken in all things that are a community with what we experience within ourselves. If we reason, we would be understood; if we imagine, we would that the airy children of our brain were born anew within another's; if we feel, we would that another's nerves should vibrate to our own, that the beams of their eyes should kindle at once and mix and melt into our own, that lips of motion-

less ice should not reply to lips quivering

and burning with the heart's best blood.

This is Love.

> Percy Bysshe Shelley

*W*hat good arms, what sweet hour will

restore to me that state from where arise my

dreams and my slightest movements?

> Arthur Rimbaud

She kindles me and sets me

aflame like fire on coal.

When I gaze on her I see such light

in her eyes and her face,

I cannot be restored

if I change or turn away

from loving her—o, lords,

how Love holds me in his prison,

Love, who conquered Solomon,

yes, and conquered David,

and the mighty Samson,

held them in his chains,

and there was no deliverance

till death, and now since he holds me,

I will have to be at his mercy.

Peire Vidal

*M*agnificent, sublime, divine sentiment!

An immortal flame burns in the breast of

that man who adores and is adored.

Benjamin Disraeli

Every object of love is a symbol of
Divine Beauty of the Spirit and therefore
has power to recall something of that
Beauty. This explains why in all love worthy
of that name there is an element of worship.

Martin Lings

No lover, in sooth, seeks union without

　　his beloved one seeking him.

When the lightning of love of the Beloved

　　has shot into this heart, know that there

　　is love in that heart.

No sound of clapping comes forth from one

　　hand of thine without the other hand.

Mawlana Rum

*I*t is not so much *what* we do but *how* we do it that transforms us.

Nik Douglas and
Penny Slinger

*E*ach day I am a better and a purer man, for I serve and adore the most comely lady in all the world, I say so straight out. I am hers from foot to head, so let the cold wind blow, the love that floods my heart keeps me warm in the coldest winter.

Arnaut Daniel

$\mathcal{F}$or love is a celestial harmony,

Of likely hearts composed of stars' consent,

Which join together in sweet sympathy,

To work each other's joy and true content

Which they have harbored since their first

   descent

Out of their heavenly bowers, where they

   did see

And know each other their beloved to be.

Edmund Spenser

O my beauty, could it be possible

To forget the night we spent together

That night was like a dream

That night we drank deep of eternal wine

That night was like a dream.

Turkish song

$\mathcal{O}$ur sexual relations are our most sacred relations.

John S. Bayne

$\mathcal{E}$very act of a lover ends in the thought of his beloved.

Andreas Capellanus

*A*borigines believe that the natural environment results from the sexual potencies of metaphysical beings and that these potencies continue to vivify the creatures and processes of nature. They also believe that the quality, variety, and intensity of human eroticism can deeply affect the surrounding life processes.

Robert Lawlor

When the land was virgin, it was dying. Nothing grew. The people asked the oracle what to do. The oracle said the Tree of Life must go to the court of that land, and sacrifice itself there. A big bird lives in that tree. Bird and tree fell. The Great Axe of the Tree of Life. Then the land grew seed-corn and yam.

Song of the Idoma tribe of Nigeria

*O*ne of the forms of love is union. It is a supreme joy, a contemplative state, a high degree, an ineffable happiness. What am I saying, it is life renewed, the exaltation of the individual, a limitless rapture, and great boon from God.

Ibn Hazm

When I consider in detail the unending marvels that a man would find in love if he but knew where to seek them, and the joy there would be in love for those who would practice it sincerely, then, all at once, my heart grows larger and I pity love when I see that almost everybody today clings and holds fast to her, and yet none gives her her due.

Tristan and Isolde

*I*f Love were to me as broad in granting
    joy

As I to her in holding a fine, frank heart,

Never for the great good (to come) would it
    vex me to be indebted;

For now I love so high the thought uplifts
    and plummets me;

But when I think how she's at the summit
    of value,

I love myself even more, for I ever dared to
    want her;

So that now I know that my heart and my
    feelings

Will let me make, with their pleasure, a

    wealthy conquest.

Even if I have a long wait, it doesn't hamper

    me,

For I stand firm and I'm put in such a rich

    place

That, with her beautiful words, she'd keep

    me full of joy,

And I'll follow until someone may carry me

    to my tomb.

                       Arnaut Daniel

As she stood and lifted those soft dark loving eyes shyly to mine, it seemed to me as if the doors and windows of heaven were suddenly opened. It was one of the supreme moments of life. Lost to all else and conscious only of her presence, I was in heaven already, or if still on earth in the body, the flights of golden stairs sloped to my feet and one of the angels had come down to me.

The Reverend Francis Kilvert

Index